Cheshire's Lost Railway

by
David James

Class C13 4-4-2T No. 67400
at Chester Northgate Station,
10 August 1953.

PICTURE ACKNOWLEDGEMENTS

The publishers wish to thank the following for contributing photographs
to this books:

John Alsop for the front cover, inside front cover and pages 7, 12–14, 21,
22, 26, 30, 33, 35, 37, 41, 42 and 46; Richard Casserley for pages 1, 2, 8–11,
15–20, 23–25, 27–29, 31, 32, 34, 36, 38, 39, 43–45 and 47; Neville Stead and
B.G. Tweed for page 48; and Neville Stead and J.E. Shelbourn for page 6.

Dunham Massey Station, 10 April 1957.

INTRODUCTION

The first public railway in Britain was the Stockton & Darlington which opened for business in 1825. This line, however, was primarily concerned with the haulage of minerals and it was not until the Liverpool & Manchester Railway formally commenced operations in 1830 that passenger services became an integral part of the railway scene.

The Liverpool & Manchester considerably reduced the costs of transporting goods from the industrial city of Manchester to the port of Liverpool, from where they were shipped all over the world. The success of this line encouraged other investors to back additional railway schemes, which led to Britain entering the 'Railway Age'. The benefits the Liverpool & Manchester brought to Manchester, parts of Lancashire and Liverpool were soon noted by prominent residents in the neighbouring county of Cheshire, south of the River Mersey.

A relatively large though somewhat underpopulated county, Cheshire was predominantly rural with a long-established agricultural base. It also had a prosperous and widely regarded salt-mining industry which was largely centred around the small towns of Northwich, Middlewich, Sandbach and Nantwich. Chester, the county town, was a wealthy and important city that could trace its origins back to the time of the Romans. Situated along the River Dee, the city held a strategic position on the main routes into North Wales and the Wirral peninsular. Thus, the county was ripe for railway development. The existence of the Liverpool & Manchester along its northern boundary made Cheshire an ideal location for new companies wishing to build railways linking up to the existing line. The first to seize this opportunity was the Grand Junction Railway.

In 1833 the Grand Junction was authorised by Parliament to build a railway line from Birmingham northwards to meet the Liverpool & Manchester. At the same time the London & Birmingham Railway was allowed to construct a line north from London Euston to Birmingham. Once completed the two lines would form a through route between London, Liverpool and Manchester.

Starting from Curzon Street Station in Birmingham (which was also used by the London & Birmingham), the Grand Junction skirted Wolverhampton before passing through the town of Stafford and then into Cheshire. There the line cut right through the heart of the county, going up to a little-known hamlet named Crewe and then on to the industrial town of Warrington, which although in South Lancashire was actually positioned astride the Mersey, right on the border between the two counties. Beyond Warrington, the Grand Junction reached up to Newton where it connected with the Liverpool & Manchester.

This final stretch of the line was to be built virtually alongside an existing railway, for in 1831, and inspired by the success of the Liverpool & Manchester, Warrington and Newton had been linked together by the Warrington & Newton Railway. This company opened a station in Warrington at Dallam Lane, while Newton was served by Viaduct Station which stood along the Liverpool & Manchester (once the Warrington & Newton opened for business it was renamed Newton Junction, becoming Earlestown in 1861). Capitalising upon its success, the Warrington & Newton added a short spur across Warrington to the Mersey in 1835 and built a second station, Bank Quay, for the handling of freight.

That same year, however, the Warrington & Newton was absorbed by the Grand Junction which was by then making steady progress on its own proposed line. By 1837 this was ready to open, but just a few days before the first trains were scheduled to run the Grand Junction's monopoly on rail transport in Cheshire came to an abrupt end.

Keen to approve more routes, Parliament granted permission for the Chester & Crewe Railway to build a link from the county's capital to meet the Grand Junction at Crewe. Up until that point Crewe had been of little significance, but suddenly it found itself at the junction of two brand new railways. The same year a third line added to the area's importance when the Manchester & Birmingham Railway began work on a railway from Manchester, and Crewe was transformed from a sleepy backwater in the centre of Cheshire to a major and rapidly growing railway centre.

Opening for business in the summer of 1837, the Grand Junction enjoyed considerable success, putting it in a strong position against its newer competitors throughout Cheshire. It was this strength that enabled the company to take over the Chester & Crewe shortly before the Chester – Crewe line was finished in 1840.

This move brought the Grand Junction into contact with the Chester & Birkenhead Railway, which that year had opened its own line from Chester up the Wirral peninsula to Birkenhead, a growing ferry port, shipbuilding and residential centre on the shores of the Mersey estuary across from Liverpool. The Grand Junction viewed the Chester & Birkenhead with hostility and tried to make life as difficult as possible for its neighbour by not running connecting trains into Chester to meet the Chester & Birkenhead's services.

The Grand Junction also saw the Manchester & Birmingham as a threat and restricted access to the station at Crewe in order to prevent that company from running trains down to Birmingham. When it opened in May 1842, the Manchester & Birmingham had to make do with operating as far as Sandbach until the disagreements between the two companies were resolved. The Grand Junction's attitude towards its competitors led to a great deal of ill feeling and bitter arguments which often needed legal action to settle.

However, all this rivalry and bitterness was put aside in 1846 when the Grand Junction, London & Birmingham and the Manchester & Birmingham joined together to form the mighty London & North Western Railway (LNWR). That year also saw the formation of the Birkenhead, Lancashire & Cheshire Junction Railway to build a new line from Hooton on the Chester & Birkenhead to join with the former Manchester & Birmingham at Heaton Norris near Stockport, and in 1847 the company responded to the creation of the LNWR by absorbing the Chester & Birkenhead. Although this gave the Birkenhead, Lancashire & Cheshire Junction control of the rail system in the Wirral it could not challenge the LNWR's dominance across the rest of Cheshire.

In 1854 another challenger appeared when the Great Western Railway (GWR) broke out of its power base in southern and western England to secure routes through Cheshire to Birkenhead and the Mersey by taking over the Shrewsbury & Birmingham Railway and the Shrewsbury & Chester Railway. This represented a serious threat to the LNWR, which responded by building the Shrewsbury & Crewe Railway in an attempt to reach mid-Wales.

Another competitor was also encroaching upon the LNWR's authority in Cheshire in the late 1840s and 1850s. The North Staffordshire Railway started pushing lines into the county from its stronghold in nearby Staffordshire, where it dominated the valuable Potteries freight business. The company obtained

Parliament's consent to build a line from Harecastle to Sandbach Wheelock in Cheshire and later followed this up by starting a link from Stoke-on-Trent to the Cheshire market town of Macclesfield via the smaller settlement at Congleton.

Despite these encroachments, the main rival to the LNWR in Cheshire – particularly in terms of local services – did not emerge until the 1860s when the Cheshire Lines Committee (CLC) was formed. This was the brainchild of Edward Watkin who had previously worked at the LNWR before becoming the General Manager of the smaller Manchester, Sheffield & Lincolnshire Railway in 1854.

The Manchester, Sheffield & Lincolnshire had already built a trans-Pennine railway from Manchester to Sheffield via the impressive Woodhead Tunnel and also had lines to the Pennine towns of Hyde, Marple and New Mills. It was now keen to extend its connections to the west and south-west of Manchester, thus breaking the LNWR's supremacy in that area. To undertake such an ambitious project the Manchester, Sheffield & Lincolnshire needed allies and through Watkin it agreed to work with its main rival in Yorkshire, the Great Northern Railway. These two companies then sponsored the creation of the Stockport & Woodley Junction Railway, which opened in January 1863. Covering a distance of just 2¾ miles, this branch linked Stockport to Marple and both the sponsors were granted full running rights over the new route, much to the LNWR's fury.

Watkin used the Manchester, Sheffield & Lincolnshire/Great Northern alliance to back other lines that were springing up all over Cheshire. In 1862 the Cheshire Midland Railway opened a line from Altrincham to the salt town of Northwich. Although backed by local figures, the line had been shunned by the LNWR so Watkin immediately stepped in to help out and thus won access rights once it was completed. The Manchester, Sheffield & Lincolnshire/Great Northern backed the West Cheshire Railway's route from Northwich to Helsby where there was a connection up to Hooton and the Birkenhead, Lancashire & Cheshire Junction's lines. In 1865 the Stockport, Timperley & Altrincham Junction Railway opened to connect Stockport to Deansgate Junction near Altrincham and once again the Manchester, Sheffield & Lincolnshire, together with the Great Northern, won the right to operate its services.

Shortly after the Stockport, Timperley & Altrincham Junction opened Watkin suggested that the Manchester, Sheffield &

Lincolnshire and the Great Northern should formally become joint owners of the various lines across Cheshire they had helped to create. However, an overseeing body would have to be established to maintain control of the various companies and ensure regular day-to-day operations ran smoothly. The idea was later backed by the Midland Railway, which had gained running rights into Manchester over the Manchester, Sheffield & Lincolnshire's lines in the Peak District from its own stronghold in Bedfordshire.

In July 1865 Parliamentary consent was sought and given for the creation of the Cheshire Lines Committee (CLC) under the joint authority of the Manchester, Sheffield & Lincolnshire, the Great Northern and the Midland. The lines throughout Cheshire set up by Watkin all came under the CLC's control, as did the Garston & Liverpool Railway which in 1864 had opened a short branch from the docks at Garston to Brunswick in Liverpool.

The CLC quickly set about extending its network across the county. Places such as Cuddington, Winsford & Over and Winnington were all eventually linked up by CLC metals, but the company's sole main-line route was the Chester & West Cheshire Junction Railway's link between Mouldsworth and Chester where a second station, Northgate, was opened in 1875.

With the LNWR and CLC dominant throughout much of Cheshire the local railway scene changed little from the late nineteenth century until the First World War. Some of the earliest stations built by the pioneer railway firms eventually closed due to a lack of customers, but others opened in their stead as the county's urban areas expanded. Little changed in terms of the actual companies involved in working services across the county, except that the GWR finally concluded an agreement with the LNWR to gain access to Manchester via a joint line from Chester to Walton Junction near Warrington. This agreement served both companies well and was soon put to use again as, over on the Wirral, the Birkenhead, Lancashire & Cheshire Junction had changed its title to the Birkenhead Railway but was quickly absorbed by the GWR and LNWR partnership.

The real change came after 1918. During the First World War the various railway companies operating across Cheshire had been forced to work closely together under Government supervision for the good of the war effort. The benefits of operating a relatively unified system had been clearly demonstrated and it was decided that such advantages should not be lost upon the declaration of peace. Thus, in 1921, when the Government's restrictions ended, a new Railways Act was introduced by Parliament which sought to reduce the 120 railway companies running throughout Britain into just four large groups. These were known as the London & North Eastern Railway (LNER), the Southern Railway (SR), the London Midland & Scottish (LMS) and the Great Western Railway (GWR).

The effects of this Grouping (as it was widely referred to) in Cheshire were highly noticeable. The LNWR became a core component of the new LMS, which also took over the North Staffordshire and the Midland which had been a member of the CLC. Another founder of the Cheshire Lines, the Manchester, Sheffield & Lincolnshire (which had by that time changed its name to the Great Central Railway) passed to the LNER, as did the old Great Northern. The GWR retained its routes to Birkenhead and Manchester while gaining considerably more influence around Chester.

For the remaining members of the CLC, independence was seen as the best way forward given their existing financial ties to both the LMS and the LNER. To award either of these groups control of the CLC's lines would have been unfair and contradictory. However, while it was to remain autonomous, the CLC did receive a new guiding committee formed on a two-for-one basis from the LNER and LMS. After the 'Big Four', as the groups became known, the CLC was rated as the fifth largest railway in Britain, while Cheshire was one of the few counties in England to be served by three of the four groups.

During the late 1920s and well into the 1930s both the LNER and the LMS sought to restructure their operations through Cheshire. Some routes were closed or declared freight-only lines while others had their number of stations reduced. However, during the Second World War the county's rail system was intensively utilised, especially to move food and fuel supplies brought ashore at Liverpool from Atlantic convoys. Troop movements also represented a major role for many of the county's lines.

By the end of the war Britain's rail network was worn out and in urgent need of fresh investment. The newly elected Labour government was committed to the idea of creating a single, unified railway under state control as a way of improving services and rebuilding an efficient system. So, in 1948, the fully nationalised British Railways came into being and the 'Big Four' were consigned to railway history, along with the CLC (which became part of the nationalised network's London Midland Region).

It was during the 1950s that the county's railway network seriously began to shrink. Falling passenger numbers (as more and more people opted to travel by motor car or bus), shifting patterns in freight haulage as a result of declining industries, and a general limitation on British Railways' budget combined to make an increasing number of lines in Cheshire uneconomical.

While British Railways chose to close some of these struggling routes voluntarily or reduce their operations to the bare minimum, it was the 1963 Beeching Report that truly started the reduction process. Throughout the 1960s, and even into the '70s, the county's rail system was systematically cut back as most branch lines were closed to passenger services. Some lingered on as freight-only lines before being finally shut as British Rail (BR), the successor to British Railways, strove to reduce its overheads.

As a result the county's once extensive web of branch lines has all but disappeared and long since been forgotten. In some locations little visible evidence remains to even suggest the permanent way once had a presence there. It is these 'lost' railways of Cheshire which this book attempts to highlight. Please note that all station closure dates refer to the ending of all services, including freight.

Neston & Parkgate Station, 2 January 1953.
Now known as Neston, it is still in service.

Cuddington – Winsford & Over

Passenger service withdrawn	1 January 1931	*Stations closed*	*Date*
Distance	7 miles	Whitegate	1 January 1931
Company	West Cheshire Railway	Winsford & Over	1 January 1931

Whitegate Station.

The West Cheshire Railway's line from Northwich via Cuddington to Helsby was approved in 1861 and later formed part of the CLC's network. Opened for freight services in 1869, the line connected with routes up to the port at Birkenhead and passenger trains were introduced a year after opening. At Cuddington a station was built to what was then the standard CLC pattern, with a stationmaster's house on the platform being a key feature. A signal box controlled the access to a nearby goods yard with sidings on either side of the line to the east of the station. It was this freight depot that served as a rail access point for the local farmers and was mainly used for the movement of dairy products, livestock and meat.

Whitegate Station, looking towards Cuddington, 26 March 1960.

The arrival of the West Cheshire led to further rural industrial development around Cuddington, notably slaughterhouses and Horner's Creamery (which is today a Nestlé factory). The station also benefited from hosting special passenger charters from Manchester once a year, which brought visitors to the annual Race Week held nearby at Tarporley. From Cuddington a single track branch line was built to the west of the station. Sponsored by the CLC and opening on 1 July 1870, its purpose was to link the saltworks on the western bank of the River Weaver at Winsford with the Manchester–Birkenhead line via a short spur at Falks Junction. The works were already connected on the east bank of the river by the LNWR. The CLC was keen to develop the branch into a two-track arrangement and purchased sufficient surrounding land to enable this to happen. It also wanted to expand the line southwards from Winsford, but this idea, along with the aim of twin tracks, was eventually abandoned due to a lack of funds and little support for the project in Parliament. Only two stations were established along the branch. There was an intermediate halt at Whitegate, where a level crossing and loading gauge had been built; then there was the terminus at Winsford & Over (named to avoid confusion with the LNWR's station in the town). Although intended primarily as a freight line, the branch provided an intermittent passenger service between Winsford and Cuddington. This was usually formed of mixed carriage and freight wagon trains which were later supplemented by a few steam rail cars.

Winsford & Over Station, 26 March 1960.

It was always easier for people to reach Winsford from Cuddington by road, so between 1874 and 1876 passenger trains along the branch were withdrawn. Although subsequently reinstated, they were once again curtailed from 1888 to 1891 and also in 1917 at the height of the First World War (they returned again in 1920). In 1930 the CLC took the decision to close the branch to all passenger services and announced that it would provide a bus link instead. The local council objected to this move and a furious legal battle ensued with the courts eventually supporting the railway company's proposal. Thus, at the beginning of 1931, the final passenger trains ran along the line although it remained in regular use for freight services until 1 June 1958. After that date only a few salt trains ran to the works at Winsford (where ICI had taken over). The goods yard at Cuddington finally closed in 1964 as most local freight had switched to road haulage. A section of the north side of the yard was later converted to serve as the station car park, while much of the south side was landscaped with trees. Two years later the final salt trains along the branch were withdrawn and the line was formally closed. Eventually, the trackbed was lifted and part of the route became a public walkway known as 'The Whitegate Way'. The disused station at Whitegate itself was converted to become a public information centre and local picnic area while Winsford & Over was later demolished to make way for a new road system. The station at Cuddington, although much altered from its earlier days, remains open. The platform signal box has long since gone, as have the semaphore signals it controlled. The track work through the station has been simplified with the single slip points into the sidings, crossover, and goods shed having all been removed.

Godley – Stockport – Altrincham

		Stations closed	Date
Passenger service withdrawn	30 November 1964	Baguley	30 November 1964
Distance	11 miles *	Northenden	30 November 1964
Company	Cheshire Lines Committee **	Cheadle	30 November 1964
		Stockport Tiviot Dale	2 January 1967
		Stockport Portwood	1 September 1875
		Godley	5 March 1962

* The line is an amalgamation of adjoining lines stretching to this total distance.
** Each line was built by an individual company which all then joined the CLC.

Northenden Station, 23 August 1952.

The close proximity of the town of Stockport in north-east Cheshire to the Manchester, Sheffield & Lincolnshire Railway's Marple line automatically suggested a short west-east branch to link the line to the town. Local residents, supported by the Manchester, Sheffield & Lincolnshire and the Great Northern Railway, formed the Stockport & Woodley Junction Railway in May 1860 to build a 2¾ mile branch from a terminus at Stockport Portwood Station to Woodley Junction where it would connect with the Manchester, Sheffield & Lincolnshire's Manchester–Marple line. Construction work on the branch was slow due to engineering difficulties and it wasn't until January 1863 that the first passenger services commenced (provided by the Manchester, Sheffield & Lincolnshire and the Great Northern). Guided by its chairman, Edward Watkin, the Manchester, Sheffield & Lincolnshire then proposed that the Stockport & Woodley Junction should be extended to join up with the Manchester South Junction & Altrincham Railway and the Warrington & Stockport Railway so as to provide a through route across north Cheshire into Liverpool. As a consequence of this idea the Stockport, Timperley & Altrincham Junction Railway was authorised in July 1861 to build a 9-mile branch from the Stockport & Woodley Junction to join up with the Warrington & Stockport at Broadheath Junction and also with the Manchester South Junction & Altrincham at Deansgate Junction near Altrincham. In August 1866 an additional junction was opened at Northenden to link with the LNWR's Stockport–Altrincham line. During 1863 the Stockport & Woodley Junction, together with the Stockport, Timperley & Altrincham Junction, were vested under the authority of the CLC. In December 1865 the first passenger trains ran from Stockport Portwood up to Deansgate Junction over Stockport, Timperley & Altrincham Junction's metals and a second station in Stockport opened at the same time. Known originally as Stockport Teviot Dale, it later changed its spelling to Tiviot Dale and quickly became the town's main railway centre due to its having a better position than Portwood's. Additional stations were then established at Baguley, Northenden and Cheadle.

During 1866 the line was extended from Broadheath to reach Skelton Junction and the Manchester, Sheffield & Lincolnshire added a new section of 2 miles – 16 chains in total – from Apethorne Junction to the south of Woodley Station over to Godley, where a station was erected close to the junction with the company's main line to Sheffield. This was transferred to the CLC's authority in August 1866. In 1875 the Midland Railway gained access to Stockport Tiviot Dale via its junctions at Bredbury and Brinnington and greatly increased the number of services passing through the station on the way to or from Manchester. This led to the decline of Portwood Station which closed to passenger services on 1 September 1875, although it continued to act as a goods depot. Trains between Tiviot Dale and Manchester improved significantly from 1879 with the opening of the Manchester, Sheffield &

Stockport Tiviot Dale Station, looking towards Manchester, 23 June 1966.

Lincolnshire's Timperley Curve which linked the CLC's line at Skelton Junction to the Manchester South Junction & Altrincham's line near Timperley Station. The service further benefited from the opening in 1881 of the Heaton Mersey East Junction just north of Tiviot Dale. This allowed direct access from Stockport to Manchester Central Station. During 1902 yet another junction was added, this time at Cheadle which gave a connection to the Midland's route into Manchester Central via Cheadle Heath. This meant that the Midland no longer had to rely on access to Tiviot Dale Station. However CLC services continued to use the station, as did most local trains. There was also a healthy utilisation of freight traffic along the entire line, especially chemical trains running via Stockport to reach Northwich and steel on its way from the works around Chester over the CLC's network. During the First World War additional sidings were constructed to cope with the sheer volume of goods traffic using the line as an alternative to passing through the heart of Manchester.

After the Grouping of 1923 the line remained under the CLC's control but there was a considerable presence in the area from the LNER and the LMS, the CLC's post-1923 parent companies. After the Depression years the line again flourished and tentative suggestions were made that part of the line from Northenden to Timperley Junction should be electrified, although this was never implemented. Again during the Second World War the line saw an increased usage and even included special POW trains running through Tiviot Dale en route from Hull to Liverpool where the captured soldiers would be shipped off to camps across Canada. During 1948 the CLC was absorbed by British Railways and despite the mounting financial losses of the 1950s the branch remained open and even played host to a number of diverted Manchester–Crewe expresses during 1956 as the main line from Manchester London Road to Crewe underwent electrification. But this was only a temporary halt in a rapidly downward spiral. Godley Station closed in March 1962 while passenger services ceased at Cheadle in 1963 with freight services also stopping the following year. Northenden and Baguley lost their passenger services the same year, although the former remained open for goods traffic until June 1965. In April 1966 Stockport Portwood closed and on 2 January 1967 Tiviot Dale ceased operating. That year later also saw the two large freight handling yards set up along the line near Tiviot Dale at Georges Road and Wellington Road become redundant. Although passenger trains no longer used the line, through freights continued to do so until they were officially withdrawn between Cheadle Junction–Woodley and Godley Junctions off the famous Woodhead route in 1982. At Northenden Junction a new Refuse Transfer Centre was established in 1981 and this has continued to provide a daily rubbish service to a landfill dump at Appley Bridge near Wigan via Northwich and Hartford Junction, while Northenden Goods Yard became home to a rail-connected cement plant.

Hooton – West Kirby Branch

Passenger service withdrawn	17 September 1956	*Stations closed*	*Date*
Distance	12 miles	Neston	17 September 1956
Company	Great Western &	Parkgate	17 September 1956
	London & North Western Joint Railway	Heswall	17 September 1956
		Thurstaston	17 September 1956
Stations closed	*Date*	Caldy	17 September 1956
Hadlow Road	17 September 1956	Kirby Park	17 September 1956

Heswall Station.

HESWALL STATION.
PERFECTION SERIES 1732.

By 1840 Birkenhead was becoming an important port on the Mersey and that year the town was linked to Chester by the Chester & Birkenhead Railway. In 1847 the Chester & Birkenhead joined with the Birkenhead, Lancashire & Cheshire Junction Railway and from 1859 this amalgamated company became known as the Birkenhead Railway. A year later it was absorbed into the Great Western & London & North Western Joint Railway. The growth of Birkenhead inspired further development along the Wirral coastline. Villages such as New Brighton and Hoylake became popular bathing resorts and in July 1863 the Hoylake Railway Company was founded to build a line from Hoylake to Seacombe and then on to the docks at Birkenhead. The company later won Parliamentary approval to extend its line to New Brighton and then on to Parkgate, a port on the western shores of the Wirral that provided a steamship link to Dublin. In the event the line was never built that far as the company went bankrupt in 1870. During 1872 a new firm, the Hoylake & Birkenhead Rail and Tramway Company, was formed to take over the old Hoylake Railway Company line and in April 1878 this company extended the route to West Kirby. In June 1881 the company's name was changed to the Seacombe, Hoylake & Deeside Railway and seven years later it combined with the rival Wirral Railway Company to establish the Wirral Railway.

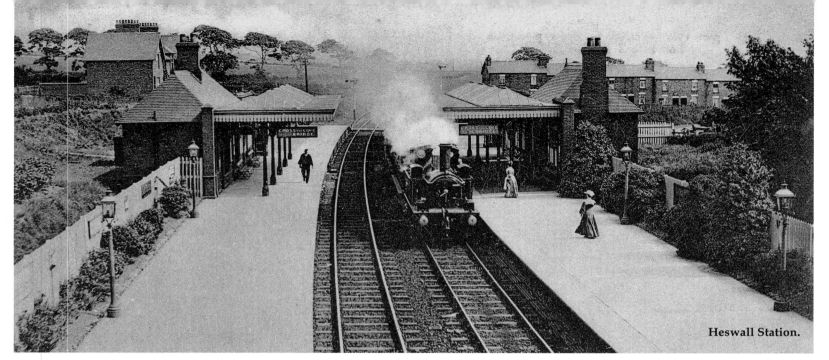

Heswall Station.

Meanwhile the Great Western & London & North Western Joint, having assumed control of the Birkenhead Railway's Hooton to Helsby branch line in 1863, was keen to extend its routes into the Wirral and on 1 October 1866 it opened a single-track line from Hooton to Parkgate with a stop at Hadlow Road close to Willaston. At Parkgate not only was there valuable revenue to be earned from steamship passengers, but there was also a considerable local coal-mining industry which benefited greatly from the railway's arrival. A new station was built at Parkgate to replace the original structure when the Great Western & London & North Western Joint extended (and doubled) the line along the western flank of the Wirral up to West Kirby during 1886. During the construction process intermediate stations were added at Heswall and Thurstaston, with Kirby Park following in 1894. At West Kirby the line's terminus lay astride the Wirral Railway's metals so services could be carried on right through to Birkenhead. Another station was added at Neston during 1896 which gave a connection to the Wrexham–Bidston line set up by the Wirral Railway (later absorbed by the Great Central Railway) and in 1909 a further station was built at Caldy near West Kirby. The branch from Hooton to West Kirby provided a useful marketing tool to encourage commuters to settle in the Wirral and it also played an important role in the transportation of local agricultural produce. After the Grouping of 1923 the LMS began providing a through coach from New Brighton to London Euston via the West Kirby–Hooton branch. The line never achieved its true potential and during the 1950s its revenues fell as the threat from road transportation intensified. Despite service cutbacks, the line continued to run at a loss until 17 September 1956 when British Railways withdrew all passenger trains from the line. It remained open for goods traffic until May 1962. Neston & Parkgate Station on the neighbouring Bidston–Wrexham line assumed the name of Neston in 1968, while the nearby stop at Heswall Hills became Heswall. Once the Hooton–West Kirby trackbed had been lifted much of its former route was taken over by Cheshire County Council to become the Wirral Countryside Park. The former station at Thurstaston became a popular picnic site while Hadlow Road escaped demolition and was preserved in 1950s' condition as a museum.

Macclesfield, Bollington & Marple Branch

		Stations closed	Date
Passenger service withdrawn	5 January 1970	Hibel Road	7 November 1960
Distance	10.5 miles	Bollington	5 January 1970
Company	Macclesfield, Bollington & Marple Railway	Higher Poynton *	3 January 1970
		High Lane	5 January 1970
		Middlewood High Level	7 November 1960

Bollington Station, *c*.1910.

* Poynton renamed Higher Poynton during 1930.

Higher Poynton Station, 18 April 1954.

The Macclesfield, Bollington & Marple Railway built the third railway line to reach Macclesfield, a centre for the local silk industry in north-east Cheshire. Prior to the railways reaching the town, local residents had to travel by coach to Chelford where the Manchester & Birmingham Railway's Manchester–Crewe line passed through. In 1845, however, a line from Cheadle Hulme (on the Manchester & Birmingham) reached Macclesfield, where a station was built at Beech Bridge on the town's outskirts. Later, the North Staffordshire Railway constructed a tunnel through the town for its Stoke–Macclesfield via Congleton line and a new station, named Hibel Road, opened during 1849.

Higher Poynton Station, looking towards Macclesfield, 4 September 1954.

Incorporated on 14 June 1864, the Macclesfield, Bollington & Marple opened for business on 2 August 1869. Initially, it was used only by passenger trains, but freight services were added from March of the following year. The line ran from the company's own terminus in Macclesfield to join up with the Sheffield & Midland Joint Railway at Marple Wharf Junction where a station was added at Rose Hill. Despite only being single track, construction of the line had been relatively slow and was hampered by the need to build a 23-arch viaduct close to Bollington, a local centre for the textile trade. An intermediate station was built there, along with additional stations at Poynton (where there was coal mining which warranted the addition of sidings from the newly constructed station to the nearby pits), High Lane and Rose Hill in Marple.

Locomotive No. 67426 at High Lane Station, 4 September 1954.

On 25 May 1871 the Macclesfield, Bollington & Marple was vested in the Manchester, Sheffield & Lincolnshire Railway and the North Staffordshire Railway as the Macclesfield Committee and three months later the new company added a connection to Hibel Road Station, which by then had also been connected to the LNWR via a line from Manchester. In July 1873 the Committee opened a new station called Macclesfield Central to the south of Hibel Road and switched all passenger services to this new facility. Hibel Road became a goods yard and locomotive depot, although the LNWR continued to run its trains from Manchester to it.

High Lane Station, 18 April 1954.

HIGH LANE

The branch's main income was derived from moving coal from the mines at Poynton and transporting local textile products. In 1873 the line was converted to double track to accommodate this traffic and six years later a new station was added at Middlewood High Level which was situated above the rival LNWR's existing Middlewood Station. During 1885 a section of track known as the Middlewood Curve was built to link the two stations in Middlewood.

Middlewood High Level Station, 18 April 1954.

The following year a spur was built from the northern end of the branch line which allowed services to run through to Buxton in Derbyshire. This route opened the way for the North Staffordshire to operate Stoke–Buxton trains via Macclesfield and also made possible a London–Buxton express to rival the service offered by the Midland Railway.

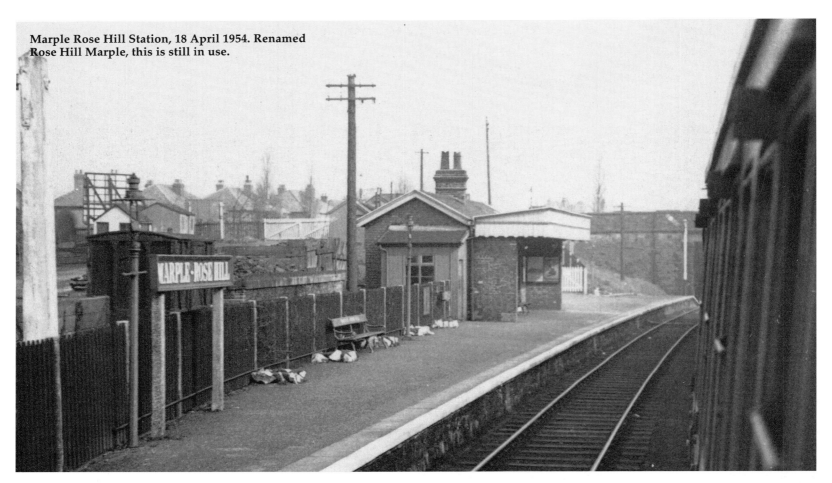

Marple Rose Hill Station, 18 April 1954. Renamed Rose Hill Marple, this is still in use.

In the 1950s British Railways turned Hibel Road into a sub-depot (coded 9C) for its Longsight-allocated locomotives, but on 7 November 1960 the station closed as British Railways opted to concentrate all trains on Macclesfield Central. The site was eventually sold off, levelled, and redeveloped. Middlewood High Level also closed on the same day as Hibel Road as declining passenger numbers and a downturn in freight movements meant that there was little need for two stations in the town. On 5 January 1970 the entire line was closed to all traffic except for a short section between Rose Hill and Marple Wharf Junction that remained in use for Manchester Piccadilly–Sheffield trains. After closure, the trackbed was lifted and in its place a public walkway known as 'The Middlewood Way' was opened.

Mouldsworth – Chester Northgate

Passenger service withdrawn	6 October 1969	*Stations closed*		*Date*
Distance	8.6 miles	Barrow for Tarvin		1 June 1953
Company	Chester & West Cheshire Junction Railway	Mickle Trafford		12 February 1951
		Mouldsworth		30 September 1968
		Chester Northgate		6 October 1969

The interior of Chester Northgate Station, 11 April 1914.

The approach to Chester Northgate, 28 August 1931.

In November 1874 the Chester & West Cheshire Junction Railway opened its line from Mouldsworth and this crossed over the GWR/LNWR joint line from Chester to Warrington at Mickle Trafford before going on into Chester itself, where, under the direction of the CLC, a new station was established at Northgate in 1875. This four-road, two-platform complex with its own locomotive depot allowed the CLC to run direct services through to Manchester Central Station via Mouldsworth, Cuddington, Northwich, Knutsford and Altrincham. Between Mouldsworth and Chester Northgate two intermediate stations were established at Barrow for Tarvin and Mickle Trafford in 1874. The line prospered until after the Second World War ended. In fact, during 1942 a new junction was added at Mickle Trafford to connect the CLC with the nearby GWR/LNWR joint line in order to reduce traffic loads on other routes in and out of Birkenhead. After 1945 passenger numbers using the two intermediate stations declined as more and more travellers opted to use motor cars or buses. A great deal of local freight was also quickly lost to the road network and the decision was taken to rationalise services along the line. Consequently, in February 1951 the station at Mickle Trafford was closed (although it remained active for goods traffic until 1 July 1963) and two years later Barrow for Tarvin was also shut.

The interior of Chester Northgate, 10 August 1953.

Passenger services continued to run from Chester Northgate Station, but in 1960 the locomotive shed there closed down. With most trains into Chester calling at the city's main station, Chester General, British Rail eventually took the decision to withdraw passenger services from Chester Northgate and from then on services operated from Manchester Piccadilly to Chester General along the former CLC cross-county lines. To allow for this British Rail had to alter the track arrangements around Mickle Trafford, which became a vital junction in the area. It remained in regular use for freight trains until 1991 when a fire virtually gutted West Cheshire Junction signal box. The cost of repairing the box and renewing badly worn track was considered too great and the route was officially closed to all services. The final passenger trains departed Chester Northgate on 6 October 1969 and the station buildings were later demolished to make way for a new sports and leisure complex known as the Northgate Arena. At the opposite end of the line the former Manchester Central site also underwent conversion into a leisure facility (after closing on 5 May 1969) and is today better known as the G-Mex Arena.

Class 3 2-6-2T No. 82021 at Chester Northgate with the 2.30 p.m. service to Wrexham, 19 September 1959.

Mouldsworth – Helsby Branch

			Date
Passenger service withdrawn	6 January 1964	*Stations closed*	
Distance	3.9 miles	Manley	1 May 1875
Company	West Cheshire Railway	Helsby & Alvanley	6 January 1964

The West Cheshire Railway's line from Northwich via Cuddington to Helsby was authorised by Parliament in July 1861. It was to connect the Cheshire Midland Railway's line from Altrincham to Northwich (opened in 1863) with the Birkenhead Railway's Helsby–Hooton line at West Cheshire Junction. Along the West Cheshire's line was a small station at the village of Mouldsworth, which became a junction in 1874 when the Chester & West Cheshire Junction Railway opened a line to Chester. As a result of this the section of line between Mouldsworth and Helsby became a branch in its own right with stations at Manley and Helsby & Alvanley. The Mouldsworth–Helsby line opened for freight traffic in September 1869 and on 22 June 1870 the first passenger services were operated. However, the branch failed to live up to expectations in terms of passenger numbers and in 1875 the station at Manley was closed (although it remained an access point for goods traffic, especially stone from the nearby Manley Quarry, until March 1961). Helsby & Alvanley was shut at the same time and for many years the line was used solely for freight movements. Helsby & Alvanley reopened in October 1936 and remained in use, though not on a regular basis, until 1944, with trains mainly using the station to bring in workers for the nearby British Insulated Cable Company's factory. To meet the needs of Britain's wartime economy and military requirements the branch underwent considerable modernisation so that it could handle heavy oil trains that ran from the refineries at Ellesmere Port to the Midlands and also supplies of food or other goods landed by Atlantic convoy supply ships at Birkenhead. Despite this upgrade, passenger numbers along the line remained relatively poor so after the war Helsby & Alvanley remained dormant until it was briefly restored to use between September 1963 and January 1964 when journey times between Mouldsworth and Helsby & Alvanley were recorded as taking a mere eight minutes. The line was finally closed to all non-freight services in March 1964 and the station was then sold off for private use after goods services ended in March 1964.

Over & Wharton – Winsford

Passenger service withdrawn	30 September 1947	*Stations closed*	*Date*
Distance	1 mile	Over & Wharton	30 September 1947
Company	London & North Western Railway		

Over & Wharton Station.

One of the shortest branch lines in the whole of Cheshire, the Over & Wharton–Winsford line was opened by the LNWR in 1882 to connect the salt town of Wharton with the main line at Winsford Junction, to the north of Winsford Station. To avoid confusion with the CLC's existing station in the town, the LNWR named its terminus Over & Wharton. Although primarily a salt line, the branch did see some passenger usage with a shuttle service operating to Hartford Station (on the Crewe–Liverpool line) five times a day each way except on Sundays. These trains were usually formed of motor coaches. Passenger duties were withdrawn during 1947, but the line soldiered on for goods traffic until October 1982 when it was closed down by British Rail.

Over & Wharton Station, 27 May 1950.

Sandbach – Northwich Branch

Passenger service withdrawn	2 January 1960
Distance	7.25 miles
Company	London & North Western Railway

Stations closed	*Date*
Cledford Bridge	2 March 1942
Middlewich *	2 January 1960
Billinge Green Halt	2 March 1942

* Between 1960 and 1965 Crewe–Liverpool trains continued to unofficially stop here in lieu of their usual stop at Winsford due to local demand.

During 1863 the LNWR received Parliament's approval to build a branch line northwards from Sandbach (where there was a link to Crewe) across the Cheshire saltfields to Northwich, the main salt mining and chemical centre within the county. The completed line opened for freight services in November 1867 and from 1 July 1868 the LNWR provided local passenger trains along the line with intermediate stops at Cledford Bridge, Middlewich and Billinge Green Halt. The branch initially prospered, especially in terms of freight haulage. Along its path were the saltworks of several well-known companies including British Salt Ltd, H.W. Morris Ltd (better known today as Cerebos Salt Ltd), Brunner Mond's Mid-Cheshire Works, Murgatroyd's, Aman's, Simpson's and Seddon's. These plants generated an enormous amount of salt traffic for the line, which was later supplemented by through coal workings from Lawton Junction to Sandbach and lime trains from Buxton in Derbyshire to the chemical plants near Middlewich, which also sent daily caustic soda services to the Crosfields soap factory at Warrington. Early passenger trains actually proceeded through Sandbach down to Crewe due to a lack of turnaround facilities at the former station, but after 1888 a new island platform was built to allow most services to terminate. In the early 1900s the passenger trains working the line became known as 'Dodgers' and from 1911 motor coaches were introduced by the LNWR to work the route. This led to the stop at Cledford Bridge opening, followed by Billinge Green Halt, and in the years following the First World War the line became useful for through services from Liverpool and Warrington to Crewe via Northwich with one train per day also using the route to provide a London–Manchester Oxford Road link until 1931.

Passenger numbers, especially on the 'Dodgers', remained relatively low as most local residents preferred to use the buses which were running far more frequently than any train services. As a result through trains beyond Northwich came to an end on 30 June 1941 with the stations at Cledford Bridge and Billinge Green Halt closing on 2 March 1942. Throughout the 1950s passenger services along the branch diminished in terms of frequency but the line became popular as a diversionary route for main line expresses. However, regular 'Dodger' services declined to just four return trips per day between Crewe and Northwich. Faced with stiff competition from the local bus companies, British Railways withdrew the 'Dodger' and on 2 January 1960 the final Crewe–Northwich service departed. Despite most salt firms having switched over to road transportation by 1960, freight services continued and even increased as oil trains started traversing the line in order to bypass Crewe. Such services originated at the refineries of Ellesmere Port before travelling over the West Cheshire lines to Northwich where they switched across to the Sandbach Branch. This then allowed them to gain access to the former North Staffordshire Railway's branch lines to travel on into the Potteries. Coal also continued to form a valuable source of business. Freight services declined after 1967 and the closure in 1971 of the old North Staffordshire line meant that the branch no longer formed part of a Crewe bypass. By the mid-1980s freight traffic had fallen to a virtual trickle, although in 1991–92 the line briefly enjoyed a spell serving as a diversionary route for London–Holyhead expresses and local Chester–Crewe workings. However, on 11 May 1992 the line was officially mothballed and has since only seen the occasional diverted service running along its length.

Warrington & Stockport Railway

Passenger service withdrawn	8 September 1962	*Stations closed*	*Date*
Distance	11 miles	Thelwall	17 September 1956
Company	Warrington & Stockport Railway	Lymm	10 September 1962
		Dunham	April 1855
Stations closed	*Date*	Heatley & Warburton ***	10 September 1962
Bank Quay Low Level	14 June 1965	Dunham Massey ****	10 September 1962
Arpley *	15 September 1958	Broadheath	10 September 1962
Latchford **	10 September 1962		

Bank Quay Low Level, looking towards Manchester, 10 April 1957.

* Arpley originally closed November 1868; reopened October 1871.
** Originally known as Latchford & Grappenhall but renamed when station was relocated in 1893.
*** Originally known as Heatley until 1857.

**** Originally known as Warburton until June 1856 when it was renamed Warburton & Dunham. In October 1856 it was renamed as Dunham and finally took the name of Dunham Massey in April 1861.

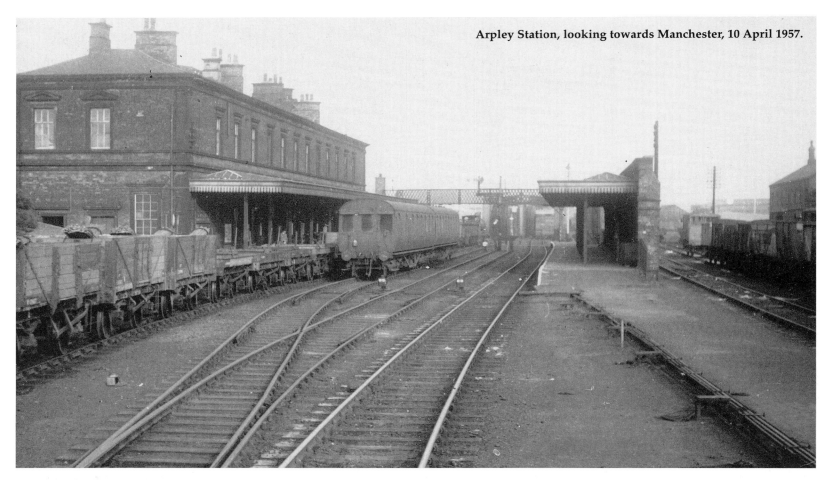

Arpley Station, looking towards Manchester, 10 April 1957.

Warrington, on the Lancashire–Cheshire border, was first connected to a railway by the Warrington & Newton Railway in 1831 and six years later by the Grand Junction Railway. During 1845 a new company, the Warrington & Altrincham Junction Railway applied to build a connection from the Manchester South Junction & Altrincham Railway's line at Timperley Junction through the north Cheshire countryside and over the River Mersey to Arpley in Warrington. There, it would join up with the St Helens Canal & Railway Company's line running from Warrington to Runcorn Gap (now known as Widnes), which had opened in 1832 and was in the process of expanding eastwards to Warrington. This scheme was later amended so that the Warrington & Altrincham's route reached Stockport, whereupon the company changed its title to the Warrington & Stockport Railway.

Latchford Station, looking towards Manchester, 10 April 1957.

In 1853 the Warrington & Stockport opened with a temporary station at Wilderspool in Warrington while the St Helens Canal & Railway Company established a stop at Whitecross on the western side of the town. However, on 1 May 1854 the two companies opened a new joint station at Arpley.

Lymm Station, *c.*1918.

The Warrington & Stockport's plans to extend to Stockport were, however, thwarted and the company had to content itself with running rights over the Manchester South Junction & Altrincham's lines from Timperley into Manchester's London Road terminus and later on into Stockport Tiviot Dale. However when the Warrington & Stockport opened for business in November 1853 a key bridge over a canal at Broadheath near Altrincham had not yet been completed and so through trains to Timperley or beyond did not start until May of the following year.

Lymm Station, looking towards Manchester, 10 April 1957.

In 1856 the Warrington & Stockport built a link east of Arpley Station to connect with the Birkenhead, Lancashire & Cheshire Junction Railway's line from Chester at Walton Junction, south of Warrington. This gave the GWR, which had access agreements in place with the Birkenhead, Lancashire & Cheshire Junction, a path through Warrington to Manchester's Exchange Station. From August 1859, the Warrington & Stockport found itself under the authority of the mighty LNWR, which having already adopted the Grand Junction's former running lines through Warrington, had redeveloped the Grand Junction's original stop at Bank Quay to become its main passenger station in the town. Having secured the Warrington & Stockport, the LNWR eventually managed to take over the St Helens Canal & Railway Company, thus giving it complete control of the line through Arpley. In November 1868 the LNWR relocated Bank Quay a short distance southwards to a new position above the former Warrington & Stockport line. As Arpley Station lay only 500 yards to the east, the LNWR saw no need to keep it open and announced its closure that month. To cater for passengers using the Warrington & Stockport route, the LNWR built two lower platforms beneath Bank Quay which unofficially became known as Bank Quay Low Level.

Heatley & Warburton Station, looking towards Manchester, 10 April 1957.

The closure of Arpley caused an outcry and led to much criticism from the local media. Eventually this negative response forced the LNWR to change its mind and in October 1871 it reopened Arpley despite the proximity of Bank Quay Low Level! The line underwent further change in 1893 when the Manchester Ship Canal was excavated.

Dunham Massey Station, *c.*1924.

The route chosen for the new waterway cut right across the railway so the LNWR was forced to close its existing station at Latchford & Grappenhall and rebuild a section of the line 100 yards to the north of its original path. To carry the line over the new canal an impressive viaduct (known as Latchford High Level Bridge) was constructed. Towering 75 feet above the Ship Canal, this crossing was reached via a 1 in 93 gradient upon which the LNWR built a new station at Latchford. This was constructed using prefabricated wooden structures which had been formed at the company's workshops in Crewe.

Dunham Massey Station, looking towards Manchester, 10 April 1957.

The line was always under the shadow of the ex-Liverpool & Manchester, ex-Cheshire Lines Committee and former Lancashire & Yorkshire routes between Liverpool and Manchester. Few services actually travelled the whole length of the line (with most terminating at Ditton Junction near Widnes) so passenger numbers were never dramatic. However, the line was useful for freight trains which used it to avoid congesting other routes.

Broadheath Station, after it was gutted by fire damage.

In September 1958 Arpley Station was closed and became a freight centre. Four years later the entire line ceased passenger operations and most of the stations along its length were closed down. Bank Quay Low Level, however, was not officially taken out of use until 1965 when the Liverpool to York mail trains that had used it were re-routed via Allerton Junction. Freight traffic continued into the 1980s, although in ever-decreasing numbers. For example, in 1979 an average of sixty or more trains travelled along the line, but by the mid-1980s this figure had fallen to just twenty or so.

Locomotive No. 42607 with the 4.05 p.m. service from Manchester to Liverpool at Broadheath, 10 April 1957.

In 1985 repair work to the Latchford High Level Bridge was deemed by British Rail too expensive to justify and the line was formally closed to all services in July of that year. A stretch of it (between Arpley and Latchford) remains in use as a shunting area for locomotives hauling merry-go-round coal trains to Fiddler's Ferry power station. The locomotives are able to run around their trains and reverse before heading up past the disused platforms of Bank Quay Low Level and along former St Helens Canal & Railway Company metals to deliver their loads.

Waverton – Whitchurch Branch

		Stations closed	Date
Passenger service withdrawn	16 September 1957		
Distance	15 miles	Waverton	15 June 1959
Company	London & North Western Railway	Tattenhall *	16 September 1957
		Broxton	16 September 1957
		Malpas	16 September 1957
		Grindley Brook Halt	16 September 1957

Waverton Station, *c.*1903.

* Tattenhall originally had two stations, Tattenhall on the Waverton–Whitchurch Branch and Tattenhall Road (originally known as Crow's Nest Station) on the Chester–Crewe main line. When Tattenhall closed in 1957 Tattenhall Road assumed its name and continued to exist until 1966.

Malpas Station.

The 15 mile-long, double-track branch line between Tattenhall Junction on the former Chester & Crewe Railway's main line and the Shropshire market town of Whitchurch was opened by the LNWR. Stations were built at Waverton, Tattenhall, Broxton and Malpas, and a small halt was established at Grindley Brook. When the line opened on 1 October 1872 services were able to run from Whitchurch all the way up to the LNWR's Chester General Station and the company saw it as a competitor to the GWR's Shrewsbury–Chester line. However, the Waverton Branch saw relatively little use and passenger numbers always fell below expectations. The line did add to Tattenhall's growing popularity as a commuter centre for nearby Chester. Served by two stations, residents of the town could easily travel by train to their areas of work while still living in the beautiful Cheshire countryside and such customers became the station's lifeblood for many years.

Malpas Station, looking towards Chester, 26 August 1954.

As with other branch lines, the Waverton Branch had relatively more success in terms of freight movements. Broxton in particular benefited from the arrival of the railway and the station there soon became a centre for transportation of fresh vegetables or fruit, local cheeses and livestock to places such as Manchester and Liverpool. Further down the line Malpas too profited from freight services, while over the county border in Shropshire, Whitchurch became a busy junction for services to Chester, Crewe or Shrewsbury and also a terminus for the Cambrian Railway's line from the Welsh borders. The Waverton Branch declined after the Second World War. Increased competition from road transport meant that more and more commuters abandoned the train while an ever-increasing amount of goods traffic switched over to the convenience of lorries. Unable to compete against such rivalry or the significantly more popular ex-GWR Chester–Shrewsbury route, the Waverton Branch was closed to passenger trains on 16 September 1957. Due to its location at the head of the branch, Waverton Station continued handling passenger trains running along the Chester–Crewe main line until it too closed in 1959. Freight services continued for a few more years with both Broxton and Malpas remaining open to handle such work. However, in November 1963 both of these were abandoned as the last freight services along the line were withdrawn. The station at Broxton was eventually demolished to make way for a car park and picnic area while the buildings at Malpas were converted into offices.

Wheelock & Sandbach – Kidsgrove

Passenger service withdrawn	28 July 1930	*Stations closed*	*Date*
Distance	6.5 miles	Wheelock & Sandbach *	28 July 1930
Company	North Staffordshire Railway	Hassall Green	28 July 1930
		Lawton	28 July 1930

* Until 1923 this was named Sandbach Wheelock, but was more commonly referred to as Wheelock.

Wheelock & Sandbach Station.

The Manchester & Birmingham Railway's Crewe–Manchester main line opened for business in 1842 and allowed for a short branch to be built from Ettiley Heath, a goods depot near Sandbach (on the Manchester & Birmingham line), to Lawton Junction on the North Staffordshire Railway's Crewe–Stoke route. The branch, which received Parliamentary approval during 1846, was supported by the North Staffordshire which viewed it as providing another route for expansion into south Cheshire from its power base in the Potteries. When it opened in 1852 the line was initially only intended for use by freight trains. A few years later, in 1866, the line was extended towards Sandbach so that it could be used as a Crewe avoiding route for goods traffic as congestion through the latter was becoming a chronic problem. However, the potential for further revenue by running passenger services along the line was obvious to the North Staffordshire so a station was later built at Sandbach Wheelock to allow trains to run between there and the North Staffordshire's Harecastle Station in north Staffordshire. Additional stops were also provided at Hassall Green and Lawton, while a new siding was built at Malkin's Bank where an important chemical factory had been established by John Tomlinson Brunner and his business partner, Ludwig Mond. Known as Brunner Mond, this company became ICI during the 1920s. The first passenger trains along the line began running on 3 July 1893 between Wheelock and Harecastle, but on average services only ever totalled three each way per day with five operating on Saturdays. Customer numbers were disappointing and on 28 July 1930 the last passenger trains along the branch were run. The line was maintained for regular freight services until 1956 and was retained until 1971 as a useful way of avoiding Crewe before finally being closed by British Rail as an economy measure. Once the branch had ceased operations its trackbed was lifted and later much of its route became a public walkway. The old station at Hassall Green was converted into a private residence that can today be seen from the nearby M6 motorway, while Wheelock found use as a mechanic's garage. Harecastle in Staffordshire, later renamed Kidsgrove Central, lasted until the mid-1960s when it was closed down as a result of the modernising of the West Coast Main Line.

Closed passenger stations on lines still open to passengers

Line/service	Chester – Crewe	Stations closed	Date
		Worleston	1 September 1952
		Beeston Castle & Tarporley	18 April 1966
		Tattenhall (originally Tattenhall Road)	18 April 1966

Worleston Station, *c.*1911.

Worleston Station, *c.*1907.

Beeston Castle & Tarporley Station, 22 August 1964.

Empty platforms as Beeston Castle & Tarporley, 22 August 1964.

BEESTON CASTLE AND TARPORLEY

Black Five 4-6-0 No. 45276 at Beeston Castle & Tarporley with a
service from Llandudno to Nottingham, 22 August 1964.

Line/service	**Chester – Warrington**	Stations closed (continued)	Date
		Norton	1 September 1952
Stations closed	Date	Walton Junction	31 October 1857
Halton	1 September 1952	Daresbury	7 July 1952
Line/service	**Chester – Wrexham**	Stations closed	Date
		Gresford Halt	1 September 1962
		Saltney	12 September 1960

Saltney Station.

Line/service	**Crewe – Shrewsbury**	Stations closed	Date
		Wrenbury	19 September 1966
Line/service	**West Coast Main Line**	Stations closed	Date
		Minshull Vernon	2 March 1942
		Preston Brook	1 March 1948
		Moore	31 December 1943

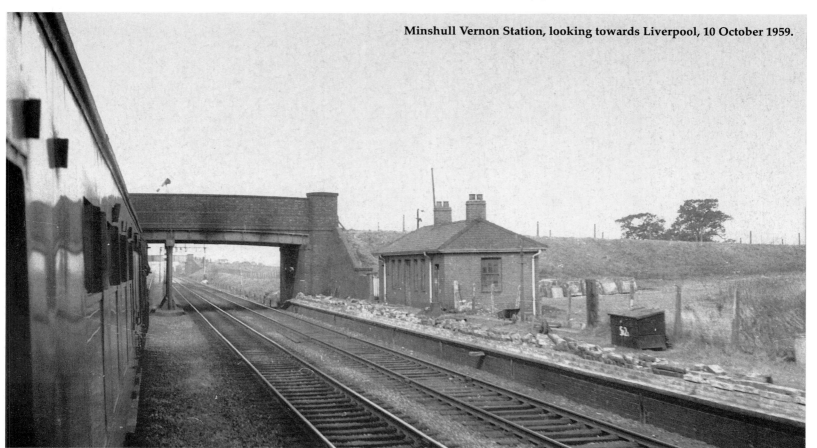

Minshull Vernon Station, looking towards Liverpool, 10 October 1959.

Class C13 4-4-2T No. 67436 with a railtour at Hartford & Greenbank Station, on the West Coast Main Line, 17 October 1953. The station was renamed Greenback on 7 May 1973 and is still in use.